Steam Memories: 1950's - 1960's

No. 78: NEWCASTLE TO CA

David Dunn

CW00735182

Copyright Book Law Publications 2014

ISBN 978-1-909625-27-3

INTRODUCTION

Conceived before the Liverpool & Manchester, and receiving its Royal Assent shortly before that railway opened, the Newcastle & Carlisle Railway opened in stages between 1834 and 1838. Twice as long as the Lancashire railway and rising nearly three times higher in elevation, the N&C was not a project for the feint hearted. Thankfully the railway and its builder's overcame the opposition of landowners, suspicious and malicious villagers, and all kinds of hostility. Today the route is as important as ever, its 'secondary route' status being occasionally waived whenever diversions on the ECML, or WCML are enforced and the N&C comes into its own.

The importance of the route came to the fore shortly after BR came into being. During the 1948 ECML Flooding diversions, the majority of freight trains to and from Scotland were diverted via the Newcastle-Carlisle line and the resultant number of trains saw a necessary reduction in the normal Newcastle-Carlisle passenger services. The diversions ran from 13th August to 25th October for freight traffic (to 1st November for passenger trains). Full passenger services resumed between Newcastle and Carlisle on 25th October 1948. Subsequent closures of the ECML have occurred since and the N&C has bore the brunt without a hitch.

Over the near one hundred and eighty years of its operation, little has changed in regard to alignment and although drastic changes occurred at the Tyneside end in the 1980s, around Scotswood and Elswick, the route is much as it was in the 1840s.

Our review of the line is fixed to the period of the 1950s and 60s' when BR steam was at its zenith, and transition of motive power and traffic patterns were taking place. We hope you will enjoy the trip which starts at Newcastle (Central) and ends at Citadel station in Carlisle.

Many thanks to the ARMSTRONG RAILWAY PHOTOGRAPHIC TRUST for the use of their material. Also, a special thank you to Colin Mountford for his excellent industrial knowledge.

David Dunn, Cramlington, Febraury 2014.

Cover **See page 77**

Title *page* **B1 No.61011 WATERBUCK runs through the cutting near How Mill with the 1.05 p.m. Carlisle to Newcastle express on 18th April 1954; note its external condition.** *R.H.Leslie.*

Printed and bound by The Amadeus Press, Cleckheaton, West Yorkshire

First published in the United Kingdom by Book Law Publications, 382 Carlton Hill, Nottingham, NG4 1JA

In early BR days there were a number of Newcastle to Carlisle passenger workings which extended beyond Citadel station to destinations such as Stranraer and Glasgow (St Enoch). Motive power for these trains was provided by Blaydon (Thompson B1s) and Kingmoor (Stanier Cl.5), but in 1954 one of the afternoon trains – the 1400 Carlisle-Newcastle (arrive Newcastle 1548) – was usually in the charge of a Haymarket A3. On 6th August 1955 St Rollox based Stanier Cl.5 No.45400 was heading one of these trains at Newcastle (Central) although the actual working is unknown. Passenger trains over the N&C were forever springing surprises regarding the motive power; in 1953 Borough Gardens based B1s took over some of the Gateshead duties on the N&C, especially the Newcastle–Stranraer (Harbour) which changed engines at Citadel. Throughout the 1950s Stanier Cl.5s arriving at Newcastle on Carlisle passenger trains rarely failed to excite as engines from sheds far and wide were used: Agecroft, Bescot, Burton, Perth, Stirling, etc. The 2.00 p.m. working was a regular turn for 64B A3s for many years during the BR era. Ironically, the Kingmoor based BR 'Clans' did not often work passenger trains on the Newcastle line, if at all, but when a couple of the Polmadie 'Clans' along with two of the Kingmoor engines were transferred to Haymarket in November 1957 to work the Waverley route, one of their number, No.72005 MACGREGOR worked the 2.00 p.m. Carlisle–Newcastle and 5.20 p.m. return on Saturday 11th January 1958. No.72005 and sister 72006 returned to Kingmoor in April 1958. *H.Forster.*

Captured on film at some time during 1958, Carlisle Canal B1 No.61222 departs from Newcastle Central with an early afternoon Carlisle express. This 4-6-0 remained loyal to Canal depot throughout its life from being put into traffic in August 1947 to withdrawal in January 1962. All of its repairs and overhauls were carried out at Cowlairs, and such was the quality of water in the area, the B1 only used three boilers with each one remaining on the engine for five years. Note that the B1 has acquired the Cowlairs valance strengthening treatment. The J71 was one of Gateshead's batch (something about the external appearance gives that fact away) which had not been in works since July 1955 hence the 'lion & wheel' emblem. The 0-6-0T transferred to Tweedmouth in January 1960 but a visit to Darlington works during the following May saw it condemned in the condition shown here. *A.R.Thompson (ARPT)*.

It is not very often that views such as this one show up so its inclusion is a must. Viewed across an untidy wood yard, we are looking at an empty stock working which has come from the Elswick direction on the west line route and is now approaching the west end of Central station with a J39 (64816) and a J21 (65103) both powering the train over the junction beneath No.3 signal box. Though undated, the period is probably circa October 1954 to 1958 on account of the J21's residence at Blaydon shed; the younger engine was also at 52C during that period. Tree foliage tells us it is certainly mid year, and it appears to be a busy time because a couple of light engines are behind the first carriage whilst another light engine is on the King Edward bridge main line south route, just behind the J39. 1955 seems to be a good bet! The photograph was taken from the site of the demolished Royal Infirmary (succumbed 1954) which became a regular gathering location for spotters' as the station was 'off limits' on a Saturday. *Malcolm Dunnett (ARPT).*

The unassuming, unpretentious, unprotected and thoroughly unkempt station at Elswick, the first station we arrive at after departure from Newcastle (Central). The notices which greet intending passengers inform them that the station is now an unstaffed halt, etc., etc. A six-car Metro–Camm d.m.u. is approaching on the Down line but there do not appear to be any customers awaiting its arrival. The date of this picture is 1966, a year prior to closure. We are looking in the direction of travel for our westbound journey and on the horizon can be seen the cooling towers of Stella North power station. *Trevor Ermel.*

Typical of Tyneside, industry was never far away from either the railway or the river. The gas works at Elswick was a case in point, and on an unknown date in the Sixties' this was the scene which visitors to the premises would come across. The saddletank was apparently named T.P.Ridley and was an outside cylinder 0-4-0 built by Robert Stephenson & Hawthorn in 1945, works number 7243, and was delivered new to Elswick in October of that year. Apart from a short loan to Howden gas works in 1951, the 0-4-0ST spent the whole of its life at Elswick and was broken up there in 1970 after closure of the plant. It appears to be somewhat neglected by the time of this visit. What is of interest about this image are the visitors at the end of the walkway who are inspecting every nook and cranny of the installation. The attire of the young boy will not go unnoticed by most of us as it was the winter 'uniform' of the era – Wellies', duffel coat, and short pants of course! Now then, would virtually unaccompanied tours of industrial plant be allowed today and what would be the age limit of participants? Would anyone be interested in such tours?? *E.Wilson.*

After Elswick station, the N&C stuck to the north bank of the Tyne as far as Scotswood where it eventually crossed the river for the only time as it strove westward. There was once a large munitions factory – Armstrong Whitworth – which stood on the north bank of the river right up to the railway, and in WW1 a station, or to be more precise a platform (it was located approximately where the rear half of the coal train is passing) was opened purely for the use of the thousands of workers at the factory. On this date in 1964 all trace of the platform/ halt had disappeared and much of the industrial asset is wasteland. We are on the footbridge located at Delaval sidings, just east of the point where the line to Carlisle had to decide which route it would take during the next six miles – north of the Tyne on the 'new' road, or south of the river over the 'old' road. J27 No.65789 is heading westwards with yet another loaded coal train which was probably bound for Stella North power station. *Malcolm Dunnett (ARPT).*

Turning round 180 degrees and pointing the camera westward, we find another J27 – No.65825 – leaving the Newburn line route and crossing onto the 'old' road at Scotswood signal box with a train of empty hoppers. To the left of the photographer, out of frame, was a small group of carriage sidings. *Malcolm Dunnett (ARPT).*

(opposite) **Moving a few hundred yards westward – you can now see the vantage point from where the previous two illustrations were captured. We have two aspects of the Blaydon route here: K1 No.62059 *(top)* is heading what appears to be a special working and has even been cleaned for the job. The date is unknown but the photographers, it seems, were out in force to record the event. *(below)* On what is believed to be the same day, a pair of twin-car, Metro-Camm., d.m.u.s run through Scotswood with a westbound service. Note the lady standing at her back gate observing the action and probably wondering what all the fuss was about; whilst a couple peer through the ground floor window of the nearest house. Another industrial installation appears just above the front of the diesel. The lone signal on the other side of the fence looks interesting. *Both R.F.Payne (ARPT).***

Taking the Newburn line to Stella North power station with a load of Ashington coal in March 1965, Q6 No.63409 runs through Scotswood and is passing the small coal yard which was situated just west of the split level, four-platform passenger station. The coal yard here, like so many small goods yards connected to BR, would soon close. Note the J27 on the lower level line from Blaydon. It is here where we temporarily leave the North Wylam loop line and concentrate on the 'old' road through Blaydon. *P.J.Robinson.*

Looking from the south (Blaydon) bank of the Tyne beneath Blaydon Bridge as J27 No.65819 runs over the bridge towards Scotswood with an Up train of empty hoppers. The date is unrecorded but the building of a new road bridge alongside the existing suspension bridge to the east took place during 1965. Beyond the bridge is the establishment of Lord Armstrong's armaments factory. *Malcolm Dunnett (ARPT)*.

Blaydon based J72 No.69024 doing what it was designed to do. Though undated, we can narrow the date down to a period in either February or March 1960, shortly after the 0-6-0T had completed a General overhaul at Darlington, when it also received this distinctive livery style; snow on the ground also helps although that 'window' could be open until May but not usually at sea level. As a precaution against the inclement weather, the shunter has the non–issue Wellies' and an overcoat come rain Mac. The BR hat finishes off the attire but note the lack of gloves! Those in the cab would be sheltered from any cold wind, having a comforting fire to rely on. The actual location of the siding is also something of a mystery but timber seems to have some connection and the Blaydon Timber Co. had their own siding in the district. Jack Teasdale, *Trevor Ermel collection.*

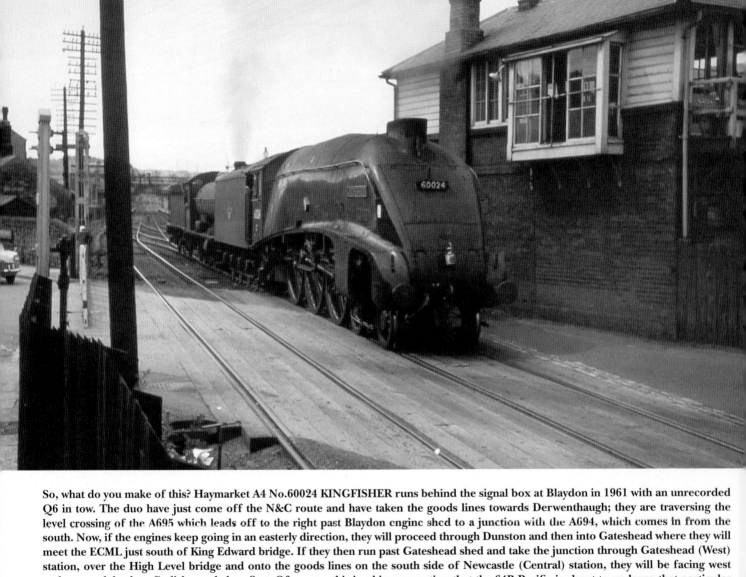

So, what do you make of this? Haymarket A4 No.60024 KINGFISHER runs behind the signal box at Blaydon in 1961 with an unrecorded Q6 in tow. The duo have just come off the N&C route and have taken the goods lines towards Derwenthaugh; they are traversing the level crossing of the A695 which leads off to the right past Blaydon engine shed to a junction with the A694, which comes in from the south. Now, if the engines keep going in an easterly direction, they will proceed through Dunston and then into Gateshead where they will meet the ECML just south of King Edward bridge. If they then run past Gateshead shed and take the junction through Gateshead (West) station, over the High Level bridge and onto the goods lines on the south side of Newcastle (Central) station, they will be facing west and can work back to Carlisle smokebox first. Of course, this is a big assumption that the 64B Pacific is about to undergo that particular journey. My assumption is based on the fact that the A4 has worked into Newcastle on the 2.00 p.m. (a regular Haymarket turn) from Carlisle. Gateshead shed was at the time undergoing rebuilding into a diesel depot and at certain periods the handling of too many steam locomotives became difficult. Blaydon shed then took responsibility for the engine off the Carlisle train but they did not have a 70ft turntable, so they sent it, along with the Q6 for signalling purposes, on that circular tour. Of course alternatives were available – or were they? Central station to King Edward bridge, into Gateshead, use the triangular layout of the junction, and reverse back to Central. If anyone knows the real reason for this unique event, please contact the Publisher via the usual channels and put us out of our misery. *Jack Teasdale, Trevor Ermel collection.*

14

A similar view but from an elevated vantage point (the footbridge) which gives a somewhat clearer view of Blaydon station, and the junction controlled by the signal box. J27 No.65788 takes water from the crane at the end of the Up platform. The proximity of the Tyne is evident. *Malcolm Dunnett (ARPT)*.

Just fifty yards or so east of the location of the last two illustrations, and a bit to the right, we are on the old alignment of the N&C. Having taken water, the Sunderland J27, No.65788 with a train of empty mineral hoppers, gets underway and has just passed Blaydon signal box and is about to traverse yet another level crossing; this one feeding a road leading to numerous industrial premises situated between the river and the main line over which the 0-6-0 is travelling. To the left is a fairly new Thames Trader lorry, from the Ford stable, which is making its way along the A695. Behind the lorry we can see the level crossing gates which were opened for the passage of the A4 and friend. Although the date is unrecorded, the J27 transferred into Sunderland on 1st April 1962. *Malcolm Dunnett (ARPT).*

An unidentified J27 approaches the level crossing at Blaydon with a loaded train of hoppers filled with industrial quality coal, destination unknown. We are looking east along the goods lines over which A4 No.60024 proceeded in 1961; about a mile further on is the bridge over the River Derwent which feeds into the Tyne at the same location. The industrial sprawl of Tyneside is difficult to discern through all the ever present gloom and pollution. The coking plant at Derwenthaugh is dead ahead, also about a mile, whilst off to the left is Blaydon engine shed amongst all that clutter; an elevated coaling plant would have helped! Once again, the date of this image is post April 1962, probably circa 1964. The present day route of the N&C follows this line from Dunston, Norwood junction and King Edward bridge; the west junction outside Newcastle (Central), and Scotswood bridge were abandoned in favour of the longer route. Perhaps the A4 was trying out the route in anticipation! *Malcolm Dunnett (ARPT).*

17

Carlisle Canal J39 No.64930 (note the 68E shed plate) makes its way home in the mid 1950s and is passing through Blaydon station.
18 *Malcolm Dunnett (ARPT).*

J25 No.65728 works a Down goods through Blaydon on an unknown date in the mid–1950s. During much of that decade the 0-6-0 was part of the Borough Gardens allocation, although it transferred to Gateshead on 14th June 1959 to work out its final years. Blaydon station was eventually one of the grander intermediate stations on the route and beneath all the grime and gloom depicted here was a well equipped station. However, BR decided to take the staff away from the place in 1969 with the resultant vandalism which inevitably followed. What the vandals didn't wreck or destroy, BR demolished and by 1977 the place was described as probably one of the worse stations on BR. The response from the corporate nightmare headquarters in Marylebone was inevitable and demolition of the remains took place later that year. Although still open, the bus shelters which pass for Blaydon railway station are something of an insult to that which went before. *Malcolm Dunnett (ARPT).*

Returning now to the 'new' line route via the north bank, and North Wylam: There were not many tunnels on Tyneside but this particular short 'bore' in Scotswood carried the appellation of tunnel. Its length – along with the date – is unknown and it was located just west of Scotswood station; we are looking at the eastern entrance where we can see restricted clearance boards, and the detritus of urban railway locations, but no daylight at the other end! *J.Mallon.*

(above) Appearing virtually the same as it did on opening day in July 1875, Lemington station required only a lick of paint to bring it up to an acceptable standard. That was hardly likely to happen between this mid-Fifties' illustration and closure in 1958 - although it wasn't unknown for BR to expend large amounts of money in order to strengthen a case for closure. We are looking east in the direction of Scotswood, and across the Tyne towards Blaydon and the high ground of Whickham. We are in suburban Newcastle!
(right) NER bridge weight restriction plate, Lemington circa 1960 – remember these bridge plates? They had so much information it was impossible to digest the contents whilst driving a motor vehicle. No two appeared to be the same but the law which protected the bridges stemmed from the Motor Car Acts 1895 and 1908. The bridge where the notice was displayed carried the A6085 over the railway; it also carried trams but they don't weigh much do they? Luckily, there are none of these notices surviving except in museums and private collections. As for all the apparently weak bridges, they have either been replaced by more suitable structures, or demolished – apparently! Both *J.W.Armstrong (ARPT).*

NOT ACACA ????? AND ????
NOTICE.
This
BRIDGE
is insufficient to carry a
HEAVY MOTOR CAR
The Registered Axle-Weight of any axle of which exceeds
THREE TONS
or the Registered Axle-Weights of the several
axles of which exceed in the aggregate
FIVE TONS
or a Heavy Motor Car drawing a
TRAILER
If the Registered Axle-Weights of the several Axles
of the HEAVY MOTOR CAR and the
Axle-Weights of the several Axles of the
TRAILER
exceed in the aggregate
FIVE TONS
NORTH EASTERN
RAILWAY CO

Silhouetted by the low midday sun, a Q6 heads eastwards near Newburn and is about to cross over the A6085 road bridge during a glorious winter's day in the 1960s. In the background is Stella North power station which became a reliant customer of BR taking in large quantities of coal every year from its commissioning in 1956. *Malcolm Dunnett (ARPT).*

A Carlisle–Newcastle express, with V2 No.60811 in charge, takes advantage of the quieter route of the North Wylam loop and is seen passing through Newburn on an unknown date. The station was closed to passengers in September 1958 so this image may have been recorded prior to that event as the platform edges appear freshly white-washed. The station buildings consisted virtually what is illustrated here, a range of timber-built structures all located on the Up platform. A small, wooden, waiting shed was the only shelter on the Down side. Like Lemington, it too was opened on 12th July 1875. *Frank Bell (ARPT). (right) J.W.Armstrong (ARPT).*

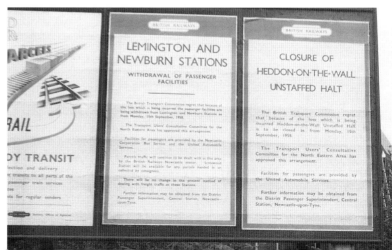

BRITISH RAILWAYS

LEMINGTON AND NEWBURN STATIONS

WITHDRAWAL OF PASSENGER FACILITIES

The British Transport Commission regret that because of the loss which is being incurred the passenger facilities are being withdrawn from Lemington and Newburn Stations as from Monday, 15th September, 1958.

The Transport Users' Consultative Committee for the North Eastern Area has approved this arrangement.

Facilities for passengers are provided by the Newcastle Corporation Bus Service and the United Automobile Services.

Parcels traffic will continue to be dealt with in this area by the British Railways, Newcastle district. Scotswood Station will be available for any parcels handed in or collected by consignees.

There will be no change in the present method of dealing with freight traffic at these Stations.

Further information may be obtained from the District Passenger Superintendent, Central Station, Newcastle-upon-Tyne.

BRITISH RAILWAYS

CLOSURE OF HEDDON-ON-THE-WALL UNSTAFFED HALT

The British Transport Commission regret that because of the loss which is being incurred Heddon-on-the-Wall Unstaffed Halt is to be closed as from Monday, 15th September, 1958.

The Transport Users' Consultative Committee for the North Eastern Area has approved this arrangement.

Facilities for passengers are provided by the United Automobile Services.

Further information may be obtained from the District Passenger Superintendent, Central Station, Newcastle-upon-Tyne.

Blaydon G5 No.67339 heads a two-coach Newcastle service at North Wylam on Saturday 3rd January 1953. This station acted as terminus for most of the passenger services on the North Wylam loop from Newcastle; it was apparently the busiest on the line. However, the future of the North Wylam route passenger services came into doubt during December 1954 when trains were cut to three each way daily. The station opened for business on 13th May 1876, a small goods yard was located at the west end of the station on the Down side. *J.W.Armstrong (ARPT). (opposite, top)* North Wylam station some thirteen years later, on Sunday 14th August 1966. By now a passenger footbridge has materialised – erected circa 1961 – courtesy of early safety laws concerning passengers. We are looking west and are about 1000 yards from the point where this line joins the original N&C alignment on the south bank of the Tyne at West Wylam junction. That junction was severed after freight traffic ceased in September 1967. *(opposite, bottom)* The view to the east on the same Sunday, with the concrete bridge centre stage. Prominent by its absence is the signal box which was abandoned and demolished on an unknown date. The passenger station, the only one on the loop since 1958, survived until the route itself was closed in March 1968, whereas the track remained in situ until April 1972. both *C.J.B.Sanderson (ARPT).*

Looking west from the footbridge at Prudhoe station in the early 1960s as a westbound d.m.u. sets out on a stopping service to Carlisle. The height of the signal box is worthy of note, the reason for its lofty elevation would be the position of the footbridge which would have otherwise obscured the view in the Up direction. Our view reveals the meagre, though still active, goods facilities which had a siding on each side of the main line with the goods shed and loading dock located on the north side of the site. Note the fitted open wagons loaded with bricks; were they being loaded or unloaded? The river is still quite wide at this point – we are now some ten miles from Newcastle (Central) – although a ford was available for road traffic which did not want to pay the bridge toll and were brave enough to chance the watery route; just beyond the bend in the river there was also a pedestrian ferry. It is interesting to note the caravans in the field alongside the river. Immediately behind the photographer, just east of the station, a large industrial complex, including a coal mine, basically marked the end of Tyneside's heavy industry. From here onwards the route became decidedly rural. *J.W.Armstrong (ARPT)*.

Stocksfield, Saturday 20th October 1956. We have covered thirteen miles since Central and we are now well and truly into the rural part of the Tyne valley. Ever since Prudhoe the route has been gradually climbing and now the gradient is reading 1 in 356. Stocksfield station opened in March 1835, one of the true N&C stations which still had two of the original canopies, one on each platform, well into the 1970s. The main station building was provided by the NER in the 1880s and was located at the east end of the Up platform just beyond the footbridge, which was also of North Eastern origin. The goods yard was accessible from both ends of the Down platform and had been worked that very morning judging by the condition of the track. Closure took place at the end of April 1965 whilst the passenger facilities are still thriving. This place had a community spirit whereby not just station staff but station users would also spend time tending to the horticultural requirements of the station. It became a stopping point during the 1950s when Sunday excursions known as 'Garden Specials' were run onto the Border Counties line during every August; when the station lost its staff in 1969, the locals carried on tending the gardens and continue doing so to this day. There were still plenty of leaves on the trees in this image but the bitter easterly winds which swept up the valley from the North Sea were not far off in time. The road on the left was the B6309 which joined Stocksfield to the A69 trunk road on the north bank of the Tyne. *L. Turnbull (ARPT).*

A Hexham-Newcastle service runs into Stocksfield behind Gateshead V3 No.67688 in the 1950s. This engine spent the whole of its life at 52A and covered nearly three-quarters of a million miles in those twenty-two years working jobs like this. The overbridge in the distance carries the A695 road from Hexham to Newcastle. *J.W.Armstrong (ARPT).*

A four-car diesel multiple unit, composed of a pair of two–car Derby Lightweight sets, departs from Riding Mill on 22nd June 1957 bound for Newcastle. This was the first year of d.m.u. services on the N&C, and sets from various private contractors and British Railways workshops began to appear during 1956 and 1957 at South Gosforth depot where a new purpose built depot was erected for diesel maintenance along the electric units. Besides these Derby-built units, Birmingham Railway Carriage & Wagon Company (BRC&W) supplied dozens, as did the Metropolitan-Cammell Co. All of course were built to what would become recognised designs which, when first introduced, had various impressions on the generations of train spotters; some loved them, others hated them. However, most of us agreed that to ride in them was very good, the view from the front compartments (maddeningly usually 1st Class only but not always) in particular was superb. Remember those miserable drivers who lowered the blinds so that you couldn't see what they were doing. Speeds of 70 m.p.h. were regularly attained by the d.m.us, and that was about the fastest most of us had travelled up to and after leaving school (the next demarcation was the motor bike for some). *R.H.Leslie.*

More than ten years later, on 9th May 1968, and the diesel set has changed to a Gloucester RWC type. The station is nearly as it was in 1957 (you will have to take my word for that) except that the N&C-built waiting shed on the Down side platform has gone. However, the original N&C station house still functions; note that the building is at the level of the original N&C platform of 1835, subsequent raising of the latter has left quite a difference in levels. The whole place was looking shoddy by 1968, the remnants of the goods facilities which had closed three years earlier, did not enhance the site. The following decade saw drastic changes taking place here and all the remaining buildings were demolished and cleared away. The bus-stop type replacements did not bring any architectural merit to the station but at least it is still open for business. *John Boyes (ARPT).*

About a mile west of Corbridge station was Farnley tunnel which was replaced in 1962 by a new cutting immediately to the south of the bore. Here, during that year of transition, BR Sulzer Type 2, D5157, has charge of a heavy unfitted coal train with the aid of a brake tender. The official closure of the 170 yard long tunnel was on 27th May 1962. *J.W.Armstrong (ARPT)*.

Corbridge station in the 1960s, with Blaydon Q6 No.63434 working through on a short, eastbound freight. The legend adorning the valance of the Down side passenger shelter leaves no one in any doubt as to where they are located; the upper and lower bands of lining appear to be somewhat different to accepted practice. The sign has been painted directly onto the boards of the canopy, enamel signs being somewhat absent on that platform. A similar canopy design was used at Bardon Mill, Fourstones, Haydon Bridge, Riding Mill, Ryton, and Stocksfield, amongst others, and was of Newcastle & Carlisle origin. Although many of the shelters stood into the 1970s, none have survived today. The small goods yard with its attendant shed edging onto the Down platform was in use until the 1960s when BR 'pulled the plug' on other installations around the system. This aspect of the station and its rural surroundings gives credence to the eighteen miles we have travelled along the upper reaches of the Tyne valley so far. *Malcolm Dunnett (ARPT).*

The new order takes over. During the week ending Saturday 17th March 1956, a pair of two-car diesel multiple units arrived at South Gosforth car sheds from the makers. These units were the advance guard of the fleet which BR (North Eastern Region) were ready to introduce on the N&C stopping services, amongst other routes. BR's investment in these railcars was heavy, a four road extension, for instance, being necessary at South Gosforth to house them – one of many such schemes. The N&C services commenced during February 1957 and within five months of that start-up, other services centred on Newcastle began. Some 134 vehicles were required to operate new the services. The new diesel trains began stopping at most or all stations between the two cities, whereas at that time most of the steam hauled through trains stopped at only two intermediate stations – Haltwhistle and Hexham. On 22nd June 1957, when this scene as recorded just west of Corbridge, an eight-car working composed of two fairly new Metro-Cammell four-car units was just pulling away from Corbridge on an evening service to Carlisle. Note the two different types of rail employed on each of the tracks – flat-bottomed on the Up and bullhead on the Down. This image, which again captures the rural setting nicely, was recorded from the overbridge seen in the distance of the previous illustration. *R.H.Leslie.*

It must be a Gateshead engine! B1 No.61012 PUKU – it is – runs over the public crossing at Dilston with a Stranraer–Newcastle express on 22nd June 1957. We are about a mile west of Corbridge amongst the fertile plains skirting the upper reaches of the Tyne. *R.H.Leslie.*

34

As eluded to at the beginning of this album, the Newcastle–Carlisle passenger expresses continued to provide both variety and surprise in the choice of motive power. Gateshead shed provided many of the A4s which plied this route; on various days in November 1955 for instance both 60005 and 60019 worked the early afternoon (1.05 p.m.) train from Central. This is A4 No.60004 on 29th August 1956 heading east through Hexham but not on one of the aforementioned workings. The Pacific, a Haymarket engine, was in charge of a diverted ECML express from Edinburgh to London which had changed its normal route because of floods caused by torrential rain during the night of 27th–28th August. Considerable damage was caused to the main line in the area around the Borders, and it was Saturday 1st September before traffic returned to anything like a normal service over the ECML. No.60004 had travelled over the Waverley route to reach Carlisle, however, some ECML expresses used the former Caledonian main line over Beattock during the closure. *I.S.Carr (ARPT).* 35

A regular in these parts, Gateshead based B1 No.61238 LESLIE RUNCIMAN slows for the Hexham stop with a Carlisle-Newcastle express on a blustery and damp – what's new? – 14th August 1956. As an aside, the former LNER Director after which this engine was named, was 36 the last survivor (died 1st September 1989) of the LNER Directors who's names were carried by B1 class. *I.S.Carr (ARPT).*

Adding to the variety! Crewe North Stanier Class 5 No.44765, with double chimney, pulls away from the Hexham stop with a Carlisle–Newcastle express, circa 1956. *P.J.Robinson.*

Yet more! *(above)* A8 No.69870 stands in one of the Up sidings at the head of a return excursion (No.100) bound for Sunderland in 1957. *(below)* Carlisle Canal shed provided this rather clean A3 – No.60093 CORONACH – for a Newcastle express in 1956. *Both P.J.Robinson.*

Obviously with time to spare, a rather grotty Gateshead B1 No.61011 WATERBUCK waits for the signal at Hexham with a westbound working on 20th September 1956. *I.S.Carr (ARPT).*

Whit Sunday 1958 saw V2 No.60935 departing from Hexham with an excursion (No.507) bound for the Lake District. The V2 was Doncaster based so has possibly been purloined by one of the Tyneside depots to handle this working. It will be noted that 36A had a similar reputation to 52A when it came to cleaning locomotives. We have a somewhat different viewpoint of Hexham from this lineside aspect alongside N&C milepost 21. Note the rail-served but rather secure Government installation on the right to which the spur coming off the main line leads to. *P.J.Robinson.*

Hexham as seen from the east end signal box in August 1977! Today, some thirty-seven years after this scene was recorded, the layout hasn't changed that much. The Newcastle bay or at least a siding on that very site still exists. The goods loop and siding on the Down side are still in situ though slightly simplified. The goods yard on the left has all disappeared but the main line is untouched. Note the engine pits still extant and a small section of the engine shed wall with leen–to attached. Finally, note the absence of Hexham West signal box! E.Wilson.

Having covered twenty-two miles exactly (give or take a yard) since leaving Newcastle, we have reached Border Counties Junction signal box (the smoke blackened nameplate simply states Border Counties). This was where the BCR left the main line to head north-westwards towards the Waverley route at Riccarton Junction. The two lines join on this south side of the infant Tyne so as to cross the river by a single line – the single line remained as the only railway although reservation for a double track was made at all the bridges over the BCR. The river itself can be seen on the left, just over the wall. Shortly after this junction we will take a short deviation onto the Allendale branch where big ideas did not become reality! *J.W.Armstrong (ARPT).*

Elrington station house on the Allendale branch in 1950 – this station opened on 1st March 1869 although the branch had opened for mineral traffic from August 1867 as far as Langley where a smelter was located. The former passenger platform runs parallel to the left edge of the illustration whilst the station house is at a right angle to the line, a situation similar to that at Langley. Elrington had a reputation as the worst performing station on the branch; the sparse population thereabouts did not help to swell the coffers. In 1911 Elrington issued just a third of what the next worst performing station (Langley) had sold. It got worse; in 1926 the booking office was closed and Elrington was demoted to Halt status. Further economic woes saw the LNER withdraw the passenger service altogether in 1930. The legacy left behind included the station houses; note that this one still has the empty booking office (bottom left window) as a reminder of what was. The building still stands in private use. Note the immaculate garden ready for inspection by either railway officials or the general public. *J.W.Armstrong (ARPT)*.

43

The branch goods train stands at the Allendale terminus after arrival in July 1950. The first goods train arrived here in January 1868. Although closed to passenger traffic from 22nd September 1930, the track and station were still in good order some two decades later but alas the final days for the branch were in sight. The train engine on this unknown date was J94 No.68059 which was a relative newcomer to the Hexham allocation (16th April 1950) though it had only come from 52C Blaydon which provided the engines for Hexham. Note the external condition of the 0-6-0ST. The last train to work the branch was the 12.20 p.m. goods from Hexham to Allendale which was worked by J21 No.65082. The train consisted four wagons and two brake vans, the latter accommodating railway officials and representatives of the press. It left Allendale at 2.15 p.m. and got to Hexham by 4.20 p.m. En route it collected a further eight wagons from the intermediate goods yards. The press interest arose from recent appeals to save the line which had been published in the Tyneside papers. After they took over the branch from 1876, the original NER plans for the line had an extension proceeding a further seven miles to Allenheads but the closure of the local lead mines and the migration of many of the local populous (in the forty years up to 1911 some 68% of the working families moved away from the area). One of our regular contributors, F.W.Hampson, was evacuated here during WWII. *J.W.Armstrong (ARPT).*

A superb view of the abandoned passenger platform at Allendale in 1950 – opened with the other stations on the line on 1st March 1869. An LNER headed notice board still adorns the building but the lack of notices is apparent. The former LNER motor lorry YY9660 (make and model unknown) must have put some miles in around this area over the years it was in operation. The daily pick-up appears to have been and gone, and a few wagons lie in the goods sidings. The yard crane had a 2-ton capacity and some of the logs lying on the ground show us what one of its main uses was up to closure on 17th November 1950. Some twelve miles from the junction with the N&C, Allendale was situated some 684ft above sea level but it was not the highest of the stations on the branch; that honour went to Staward which was some one hundred and thirty odd feet higher! *J.W.Armstrong (ARPT).*

Back on the main line, we come to Fourstones which was located 25 miles from our starting point – not quite half-way. Opened in 1837, Fourstones station was something of a gem amongst stations. The station house, with its distinctive T-shaped and rounded extension, stands to the rear of the signal box; the house is still in residential use today (is it Listed?) whilst the signal box is one of those which are no longer operational. *John Boyes (ARPT).*

The delightful setting of Fourstones station, allegedly on 20th October 1956 but the foliage and blooms point to a period some weeks earlier. We are looking west with all the original facilities in situ. Dating from 1837, Fourstones was built to replace two other nearby stations which were planned to be built at Allerwash and Warden but were not proceeded with. We are looking at the NER station building of 1880 which was built to replace the 1837 facilities just illustrated, and located behind the signal box. Floral displays seem to be the order of the day, with both platforms bedecked. Note the goods shed, platform and sidings at the west end of the Up platform. *L.Turnbull (ARPT).*

The western end of Haydon Bridge station circa 1960; the signal box is prominent, although that water column appears to be trying to grab the attention. Besides the road vehicle crossing, passengers also used a level crossing to change platforms, etc., and the wooden planking nearest served as the only means of crossing the railway for many years into the BR era. The signal box must predate the two-storey station building on the Down side, its stone design fitting in nicely with the late 1830s architecture of the original station whereas the two-storey station building was constructed in 1876 and was built from bricks. *E.Wilson.*

Virtually halfway between Newcastle and Carlisle, on the north side of the railway at Bardon Mill, was a small colliery (nothing unusual in this part of the world but its youth, compared with other collieries adjacent to the main line, was unusual, as also was its location so far west at this late period of the NCB). Like many of the smaller 'pits' in this part of the Durham/Northumberland coalfield, it was a drift mine and employed no more than three hundred men during its most productive period. However, its productive lifetime of twenty-five years, for a drift mine, was quite long. In that time-span it was producing approximately 150,000 tons of saleable coal each year (about 500 tons every working day). Much of the coal left by rail, rather than via the A69 trunk road, and to help marshall and shunt the hopper wagons a four-coupled, outside cylinder, saddletank was employed and can be seen in this 9th May 1968 illustration. Built by Hawthorn-Leslie in 1906 (works No.2660) the engine in view (No.C19 outside its shed) was replaced at sometime in 1970, or beforehand, by a younger 0-4-0ocST which had joined the National Coal Board fleet (their No.40) from Andrew Barclay's in 1950 (works No.2280). The mine closed in 1973. *John Boyes (ARPT).*

This is the west end of the 202 yard long Whitchester tunnel – also known as Haltwhistle tunnel – on 16th May 1959. Now thirty-six miles from Newcastle, we are climbing a 1 in 332 incline which does not seem to be testing the Thompson B1 too much. No.61239 is hauling the 12.20 p.m. Newcastle (Central)–Carlisle and is now more than halfway to its destination. In just over a mile will be the stop at Haltwhistle, then five miles of fairly easy climbing before virtually closing the regulator for the downhill run to Citadel. Note that the Carlisle Canal based B1 has been through Cowlairs works at some point in its short life, and been fitted with the curved valances on the underside of the running plate – a speciality of the Glasgow workshop in BR days. *R.H.Leslie.*

We have arrived at Haltwhistle to find the same B1, No.61239, departing for Carlisle with another Newcastle train some years earlier in late October 1956. This panoramic view of the western end of the station reveals the goods facilities on the Up side, and the locomotive facilities at the western end on the Down side, known as Haltwhistle Station Yard. Not only were engines from the Alston trains serviced here but those off the Carlisle to Haltwhistle 'stoppers' would clean their fires, top up their tanks and turn here too. The 46ft 4in. turntable can just be seen in amongst the trees on this side of the 30ft engine pit. During LNER days C15s from Carlisle Canal shed would often work local trains as far as Haltwhistle. Latterly other rare engines have turned up courtesy of Canal shed; N2 No.69564 arrived on the morning pick-up goods (normally a J39 duty) on 17th September 1957. Meanwhile, in the Alston branch platform a three-carriage train awaits passengers from the Newcastle train which have probably already boarded; it looks like a J39 in charge today. It is not readily appreciated from this aspect that Haltwhistle had staggered platforms linked by the footbridge. The River South Tyne meanders past the town and will eventually (in 13 miles or so) meet the North Tyne to become the Tyne proper. Not visible from here is the bridge which crosses the river carrying the Alston branch. *R.H.Leslie.*

The signal box looks smart, the footbridge also looks rather smart but Haltwhistle has lost some of its charm and certainly its branch line. The date is unknown but the box dates from 1901 and it was replaced from 1993 by a modern prefab structure on the Up side. *Paul Moore.*

Three decades earlier! K1 No.62030 runs through Haltwhistle with coal empties on 12th April 1952. It was downhill all the way for the 2-6-0 from hereon. *J.W.Armstrong (ARPT).*

(above) Looking across a rather sedate River South Tyne, we have a view of Haltwhistle viaduct from the north bank on 20th October 1956. *L.Turnbull (ARPT). (below)* Having successfully traversed the viaduct, Blaydon Cl.3 No.77014 works its way to Alston on 16th May 1959; note that the train now consists a BR Mk.1 carriage and an ex-LNER vehicle. Following reorganisation of train services on the branch to Alston from July 1954, all traffic, both passenger and freight was handled by one engine in steam, usually a BR Class 4MT from Blaydon. It was reported that: 'An ex-Great Eastern 3-coach corridor set labelled 'Conductor Guard' is now in use at the branch and it is believed that tickets are to be issued by the guard from at least two intermediate stations which are to become halts.' One year later, on 8th August 1955, BR Std. Cl.3 No.77011 was working the branch and had two LNER corridor carriages. Change was constant. *R.H.Leslie.*

With diesel multiple units now working the Alston branch – how much easier that must have become for all concerned – we have a two-car unit at Haltwhistle on 14th October 1961. Both river crossings are in view with the waterway looking very calm once again. *Malcolm Dunnett (ARPT).*

The Alston branch train on Saturday 12th April 1952; the crew of G5 No.67315 are doing the honours for the cameraman. This engine was allocated to Alston for a number of years (29th May 1940 to 7th June 1953) having come initially from Rothbury and then, in BR days, moving to Blaydon. The excellent external condition of the 0-4-4T is not necessarily due to the labours of the crew because No.67315 had just returned from a three–week long Light Intermediate overhaul at Gateshead so was probably repainted then. *J.W.Armstrong (ARPT)*.

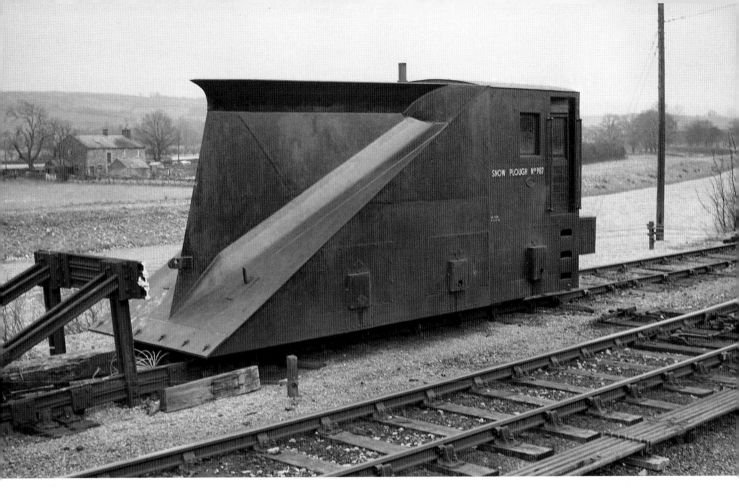

Just in case! Heavy duty snowplough No.987 stands in a siding alongside Haltwhistle station on 6th April 1963. Built on a tender chassis, and with a fully enclosed cabin, complete with stove, the plough looks quite formidable but it has just had one of its busiest winters working both the branch to Alston and the main line. Its summer residence was on a spur outside the engine shed at Alston. *A.Ives (ARPT).*

Gateshead B1 No.61014 ORIBI arrives at Haltwhistle circa 1952 with a Newcastle–Carlisle service. Note the station house which appears to be larger than others on the route so far seen. *J.W.Armstrong (ARPT).*

Two views of the locomotive area at Haltwhistle on 12th April 1952 with *(above)* V2 No.60959 running into the station with an Up express whilst G5 No.67315 nestles over the pit, and *(below)* the four-coupled tank and its crew posing – turntable to the left, pit to the right. Now who was that third member? both *J.W.Armstrong (ARPT)*.

Time to visit the Alston branch: *(above)* J39 No.64853 departs from Haltwhistle for Alston and is seen crossing the river South Tyne viaduct on 27th October 1956 with three carriages in tow. It was reported that on Saturday 18th August 1956, the 1.47 p.m. Haltwhistle–Alston train was worked by J39 No.64814 (52C) with three comparatively new ex-LNER carriages in place of the ex-GER set. Could these be them? *(below)* Same engine, same viaduct, different date – 22nd June 1957, and a different set!!! *Both R.H.Leslie.*

The compact terminus at Alston circa 1959: A special working d.m.u. is hogging the passenger line whilst a BR Cl.3 is alongside the coaling stage. We have travelled some thirteen miles from Haltwhistle, climbed exactly 500ft from our starting point there, and stopped at four intermediate stations: Featherstone Park, Coanwood, Lambley, and Slaggyford. The railway from Haltwhistle was opened throughout to Alston in November 1852 although sections from Alston to Lambley had already been open for some months. The terminus at Alston included a one-road engine shed which housed the branch engine/s until diesel units took over the passenger workings from September 1959. After years of trying to close the branch but unable to because of the combination of bad winters and poor roads, BR were finally able to rid themselves of this loss-making branch in 1976 when better road facilities were installed. *R.F.Payne (ARPT).*

(above) The station throat at Alston with G5 No.67315 running round its train on 12th April 1952. Note the snowplough laid up for the summer season; that appears to be a different model to the one shown at Haltwhistle. *(below)* The station on the same day with the 0-4-4T now coupled up to its train ready for the run back to Haltwhistle. *both J.W.Armstrong (ARPT)*.

Back onto the main line and just to the west of Haltwhistle, where the A69 trunk road skirts the N&C for more than two miles, you could sit by the roadside all day long and view the railway. On 19th May 1956 B16 No.61469 was taking it easy after the climb up to Gilsland with this train of pipes which had originated in Workington. The 4-6-0 was a newcomer to this route having been allocated to Blaydon for just six days prior to working this trip; less than two months later it returned to Heaton and then to pastures anew. No.61414 came with No.61469 but was gone from Blaydon in June. However, during LNER days Nos.61427 (932), and 61436 (2365) were residents of Blaydon from July 1924 to September 1937 during which period they would have worked N&C metals. No.61448 (2377) joined them for the final months of 1937, and that was it. The sum total of B16s allocated to the N&C. No wonder it was reported that a couple of the class worked the route for a short period during the summer 1957: 6th July 1957 – 'A shortage of motive power at Gateshead resulted in two York B16s being used on the Carlisle line. No.61465 arrived on time with the 12.29 p.m. from Ayr whilst No.61460 followed, with a parcels train from Carlisle.' For the record, No.61469 started its BR life as No.61400 but was renumbered on 21st December 1949 to give that number up to a new Thompson B1. *R.H.Leslie.*

In one of those rare instances where the N&C deviates from the generally east-west axis, we are looking virtually due south along the Greenhead station platforms on 20th October 1956. To the left is the Up side with the booking office combined with the waiting room. Just behind the aforementioned building is the former engine shed provided by the N&C for the opening of the line but closed on an unknown date. That it was still surviving in good condition one hundred and twenty years later is quite remarkable; it was reported as still standing at the turn of the millennium. The track behind the signal box led to the engine shed and separated the station house from the Up platform; the goods facilities were also behind the signal box. The Down platform has a N&C waiting shed in this view but look at the cottage at the roadside; that too was part of the platform layout with the lower floor on the platform and a first floor entrance at street level. Although the station is no longer in existence, having closed in 1967, the house linking the street and the erstwhile platform survives. *L.Turnbull (ARPT)*.

The rather 'posh' Gilsland station, or at least part of it, in October 1966. Some forty-two miles from Newcastle, we are now at the highest station, indeed just about the highest point, on the N&C at circa 550 feet above sea level which doesn't seem very high in Pennine terms but that is the fact. It seems incredible that anyone would want to build a station here but that's what the N&C did in 1836. Just about a mile away was a spa (the eighteen-hundreds' equivalent of a multi-screen cinema where you could stay if you had the money) known as Gilsland which eventually gave the station its name. Until 1869 the station was known as Rose Hill and, as far as the Roman's were concerned, this station would have been in Scotland – or at least in the uncivilised part of Albion – because Hadrian built his wall immediately to the south of the station or the site which was to become the station nearly two thousand years later! The oil lamp in the foreground is attached to one of the numerous cast iron posts which supported a large area of roof in front of another section of station buildings. Note that the original building has been attacked by vandals who fitted two dormer windows on an otherwise immaculate design. The spa certainly helped receipts at this place but time changes things and the spa later became a convalescent home. Consequently the crowds dispersed. Closure came in 1967 but most of this range of station buildings survives today. A good friend of mine, Mr Elsworth Brooks (Alan) contemplates the scene. *E. Wilson.*

Besides being the junction for the one-and-a-half-mile branch to Brampton Town, Brampton Junction was also the junction for another much longer – goods only – line, which set out in an easterly direction to tap the mining interests tucked around the bottom of Tindale Fells. Brampton Jct. was initially named Milton when opened in 1836 but in 1870 it was renamed. In this circa 1952 view B1 No.61238 LESLIE RUNCIMAN is running through with an express for Carlisle. As can be seen, the original station buildings were all ranged on the Down platform and at a lower elevation, subsequent raising of the platform has brought the level up to window cill height. The platform from where the illustration was recorded was both the N&C Up platform and the Brampton Town branch platform before the branch closed in 1923. This station survives but in a much modified state. *J.W.Armstrong (ARPT)*.

Running down hill with ease, and crossing the short viaduct known as Gelt Bridge, B1 No.61222 heads westward with a Newcastle–Carlisle working on 12th April 1958. We are approximately halfway between Brampton Junction station and How Mill station where the River Gelt and two minor roads are crossed. The river rises on nearby Geltsdale and is a tributary of the Eden. *R.H.Leslie.*

Two years earlier, at the height of summer growth on Monday 6th August 1956, V2 No.60840 traverses the viaduct at Gelt Bridge with the 8.45 a.m. Carlisle (Citadel)–Newcastle (Central) express. *R.H.Leslie.*

Just a little further west of the last location, in April 1958 and with the afternoon sun out, we find a grotty looking K1, No.62029 of Blaydon shed, keeping a heavy coal train in check. It is easy to forget just how much coal was moved by BR and the Newcastle-Carlisle line saw its fair share; most of it westbound as here. The line remains in this cutting for about a mile; note how wide the floor of the cutting is at this point, necessary because of the strata consisting mainly sand; originally a tunnel was planned by the N&C but instead this cutting, which in places reached a depth of 110 feet, was deemed the most practical solution. At its widest point some 305 feet separate the two high points of the cutting. *R.H.Leslie.*

A3 No.60079 BAYARDO, a Carlisle Canal Pacific, has charge of the 12.20 p.m. Newcastle-Carlisle express on Saturday 1st June 1957. The train is at the western end of the cutting near a place called Cowran, the depth now starting to show. It was something of a 'whopper' amongst the railway cuttings of Britain. Retaining walls line some sections of the excavation, as here. *R.H.Leslie.*

Another view of the dramatic earthworks at Cowran; this shows the extent of the retaining walls. Blaydon based B1 No.61238 LESLIE RUNCIMAN, which was recently ex–works, fights the grade with an eastbound freight on Saturday 12th April 1958. *R.H.Leslie.*

An eastbound anhydrite train with Blaydon K1 No.62006 at its head tries to leave How Mill behind on 12th January 1957. The 2-6-0 is tackling the last of four miles of 1 in 107 – about the steepest it gets on the N&C – after which it settles to a more modest 1 in 295, 171, and then a luxurious 1 in 601 for a mile. The fireman is looking out from his side of the cab so appears up-to-date with his tasks but there are a few miles yet before he can really relax after Greenhead. *R.H.Leslie.*

A busy moment at How Mill station as a Newcastle–bound express passes a westbound mixed freight. The latter is hauled by Q6 No.63441, one of Blaydon's stud and a regular performer over the N&C line. The station here had staggered platforms, built of timber, with a level crossing separating the two; the east end of the Up platform can just be seen behind the brakevan of this goods train. Dating from July 1836, the nearest village was about a mile away to the north and was called Hayton (pop.1210 in 1935); up to the internal combustion engine getting established, Hayton and the surrounding villages generated enough traffic for the station to thrive but post-war receipts were not enough. How Mill was closed from Monday 5th January 1959, along with the goods yard. *R.H.Leslie.*

Heads Nook station was late opening in N&C terms and didn't become operational until September 1862. Facilities were minimal with a waiting shed at the east end of the Up platform, and booking office and waiting shed combined at the west end of the Down platform. When this image of B1 No.61100 working the 12.15 p.m. Stranraer–Newcastle express was recorded on 23rd July 1960, the station still had another seven years of operations in front of it, a lot more than the Gateshead (but note the 52C Blaydon shed plate still attached) B1 could look forward to. The 4-6-0 has at least ten vehicles in tow, all from various vintages. This station was not one of those which has survived to fight another day and all remains except the station house (not in frame here) have been swept away. *R.H.Leslie.*

The goods yard at Heads Nook was located a few hundred yards west of the passenger station at a place described as Stonerigg. On 1st January 1957 Blaydon allocated K1 No.62029 leads a westbound mixed freight past the yard. Note the coal sacks hanging out to dry on the fence. The wooden-bodied wagons serving the coal siding look the worse for wear and due for renewal; hundreds of thousands of 16–ton steel bodied mineral wagons had already been constructed by this date but none had materialised here yet. This facility was active until 5th April 1965. *R.H.Leslie.*

Blaydon K1 No.62027 runs off the Eden gorge viaduct and into Wetheral station on Bonfire Night 1955 with a westbound freight consisting mainly, it appears, of loaded coal wagons. The station at this location was provided for the opening of this section of the N&C in July 1836. A section of the single storey station building, with its glazed verandah, is visible on the left, Up side. Note the timber decked footpath provided on the north side of the viaduct parapet – the BR notice at this end stated that 'persons must not ride cycles over the bridge.' The nearest road vehicle crossing of the River Eden was over a mile away to the north where the A69 trunk road traversed Warwick bridge; a pedestrian ferry just to the south of the viaduct was another means of crossing the river for those without a head for heights. For the record, the viaduct is 95ft high and consists of five arches with a total length of 188 yards or 564 feet! *R.H.Leslie.*

On the same day, the 1.05 p.m. Carlisle-Newcastle express thunders through Wetheral (speed restrictions of about 45 m.p.h. applied through the station area and beyond the viaduct) with Gateshead B1 No.61100 in charge. This illustration affords us further views of the station with a North Eastern built waiting room on the right whilst the original station house stands to the west. The signal box was located on the embankment above the Down platform just about opposite to the station house. Although equipped to handle goods, and having a 2-ton capacity yard crane, that particular facility had been withdrawn on the previous 1st April, which was quite early for the N&C as a whole. Closure of the passenger station took place in January 1967 but 'people power' eventually prevailed and the station was re-opened in October 1981. Much of the original structure remained and luckily BR showed some common-sense and simply refurbished the old buildings although local influence had some bearing on the decision. *R.H.Leslie.*

We approach Carlisle just as a four-car d.m.u. heads eastwards for Newcastle. The date is 17th May 1959 and the location is Durranhill or Durran Hill as some schools prefer. Before us lie the yards of the former Midland Railway on the left, and the ex–NER yard on the Up side. The industrial belt on the east side of the city is represented by a factory resplendent in its newness whilst beyond were the premises of crane makers renowned the world over. On the left stood Durran Hill engine shed, a square roundhouse which was officially closed in the 1930s but remained in use as a store, engine shed, and repair shop until the 1960s! On the right, at the western end of the yards lay another engine shed, another square roundhouse even – London Road of NER origin – which consisted two adjoined roundhouses dating from 1881 and 1890 which were closed for engine purposes in 1933 but became a wagon shop thereafter. They were standing until the end of the 20th Century and can be seen immediately above the second car of the d.m.u. The N&C opened their engine shed here in 1836, on the site just in front of what became the NER shed, but it was destroyed by fire in April 1864 and replaced by another, this time of NER design. *R.H.Leslie.*

So, with our journey nearly completed, we join Canal A3 No.60068 SIR VISTO on an empty carriage working into Citadel station on a rather frosty Saturday 10th January 1959. The stock will form the 2.00 p.m. express to Newcastle but what the motive power will be is uncertain. We have travelled some sixty miles, gone straight up a hill and down the other side without too much bother. We have deviated over two branch lines, and traversed a loop line which once offered an alternative to Tynesider's. What we haven't done is negotiate the new longer section of the route now taken by Newcastle–Carlisle trains over the Gateshead and Blaydon line but that didn't exist as such in the 1960s where our remit ends – please don't write in regard to the Hexham 1977 illustration; its simply there for the record! *R.H.Leslie.*

In July 1952, a Saturdays Only (1.50 p.m.) Carlisle–Newcastle service stands ready for departure from Citadel station with Alnmouth D20 No.62371 in charge. This image proves once again that there certainly was a variety of motive power used for the N&C passenger trains. Time keeping however varied accordingly with the power and condition of the engine, and the load. Note that the 4-4-0 has both a Tweedmouth 52D shedplate and the Alnmouth legend painted on the bufferbeam. After Nationalisation the D20 allocation at Tweedmouth grew to more than a dozen but usually all but one were sub-shedded at Alnmouth. Many of the class which survived into BR days ended up at Alnmouth shed, including 62371 which returned to Tweedmouth on 15th March 1953, re-allocated to Gateshead on 7th June 1953 then transferred to Almouth on 4th October 1953. It was condemned in October 1954, apparently with the BRITISH RAILWAYS legend still adorning the tender sides! *R.H.Leslie.*